Damien

Damien

Aldyth Morris

THE UNIVERSITY PRESS OF HAWAII

Honolulu

Library of Congress Cataloging in Publication Data

Morris, Aldyth, 1901–
  Damien.

  Bibliography: p.
  1. Damien, Father, 1840–1889—Drama. I. Title.
PS3563.087397D3   812'.5'4   79–22915
ISBN 0-8248-0693-X

To my husband

Song of the Chanter Ka-'ehu

What will become of Hawai'i?
What will leprosy do to our land—
disease of the despised, dreaded alike
by white or brown or darker-skinned?

Strange when a man's neighbors
become less than acquaintances.
Seeing me they drew away.
They moved to sit elsewhere, whispering,
and a friend pointed a finger:
"He is a leper."

I bowed my head.
I knew it was true.
In my heart I hugged my shame.

Word reached the medical authorities.
The doctors sent the military to fetch us.
We were caught like chickens, like cattle herded
along roadway and country lane.
Then they paraded us before the Board of Health
but there was no health in that Board for such as we.
Examining doctors eyed us, squinted this way and that.
More fingers pointed Diamond Head way:
"You go to Kala-wao!"

Again the militia took over.
Soldiers escorted us to the wharf for farewell.
Prisoners, we were marched aboard,
victims of leprosy, branded for exile.
Abandoned, cut off from family and dear ones,
we were left alone with our grief, with our love.
Rain of tears streamed from leper eyes.
Leper cheeks glistened with raindrops in the sun.
Never again would we look upon this land of ours,
this lovely harbor town.

Quickly the sails were hoisted.
Ropes dangled from the foremast,
tails of wild animals writhing,
whipping in the channel breeze.
The *John Bull* drew anchor.
In the stern the rudder turned.
So sailed we forth to dim Moloka'i Island,
enshrouded in fog.

So ends my song and this refrain.
What will leprosy do to my people?
What will become of our land?

This chant, written originally in Hawaiian, is the last known composition of a composer, chanter, and
hula master, who became a leper and died at the Kalaupapa settlement on Moloka'i.

Damien was first produced by the University of Hawaii Department of Drama and Theatre, Glenn Cannon chairman, and opened at their Kennedy Theatre, 18 June 1976, starring Terence Knapp as Damien.

CREDITS

Production assistant	Cecilia Fordham
Set design	Richard C. Mason
Lighting design	Linda Breden
Costume	Sandra Finney
Technical direction	Mark Boyd
Crucifix figure	Kalanikoa Lum
Sound recordings	Roseann Concannon and Joel Aycock
Sound operation	Gerald Kawaoka

In May 1977, Hawaii Public Television, Mary Bitterman executive director, began taping *Damien* for television, with Terence Knapp in the role of Father Damien. The original stage script was retained and restaged for television by Executive Producer/Director Nino J. Martin. It was first aired in Hawaii in September 1977 and nationally on PBS Stations in January 1978. It has received nationwide recognition, including the George Peabody Award, Christopher awards to author and director, Corporation for Public Broadcasting Honorable Mention for Drama, National Association of Educational Broadcasters Award for Art Directing, and Ohio State University Award.

CREDITS

Producer/Director	Nino J. Martin
Lighting Director	Mikel Neiers
Art Director	Mel Farinas
Musical Director/Composer	John Bode
Assistant Director and Script Coordinator	Gerri Char
Production Manager	Don Dresser
Unit Manager	Larry Sichter
Crew Chief	Wade Couvillon
Sound Engineers	Jim Walter and Steve DeFeo
Engineers	Barry Albright and Ed Tanabe
Make-up	Charles Enos Martin
Production Technicians	Gary Chun, Mike Munemitsu, Lester Iwamasu, Pat Sexton
Music Performers	Keola, Kapono, and Nona Beamer
Crucifix figure	Kalanikoa Lum
Costume	Sandra Finney

Terence Knapp as Damien

Damien

The set for the University of Hawaii production was designed by Richard C. Mason and provides the various acting areas called for in the play.

An open space from downstage right to left for the actor when he is speaking directly to the audience.

Stage right, an old rocking chair and low table to suggest Father Damien's living quarters at the leper settlement.

Upstage center, a bank of flickering votive lights behind a large black box affair that could be either an altar or a coffin, to designate the cathedral area.

Midstage center, a neutral area with a smaller black box on which the actor may lean, sit, or rest his foot.

Stage left, an open area representing the offices of the Board of Health, and giving directly onto a runway thrust deep into the audience. The runway serves as the landing place at the Leper Settlement.

Other neutral areas may be defined as needed by lighting.

High overhead, dominating the stage, is a huge crucifix.

The action of the play takes place during a journey from the Hawaiian island of Moloka'i to Louvain, Belgium, in 1936.

ACT ONE

The curtain is always up. As the house lights go down the offstage sound of a Hawaiian chant is heard. As the chant comes to an end the stage lights dim almost to darkness and the voice of Father Damien is heard.

Damien: This is the time of day I always hear them. Dusk. When the sun's gone down but there's still light enough to recognize a face. Lepers—forty or fifty of them at a time—marched between armed guards, from Kalihi-kai down King to Bishop, and on down Bishop to the waterfront, where small boats wait to take them to that larger boat anchored farther out—the leper boat. It always leaves at dusk on Monday, and travels in the dark to dump its human cargo before the sun comes up. This is the time of day I hear their muffled step, the mourning sounds that follow after, the haunting farewell chant, the anguished cries of separation, then the shrill whistle as the leper boat moves off across the water.

(Stage lights up slowly to reveal Father Damien in priestly hat and cassock. He half stumbles downstage center. To the audience)

Damien: My feet have always been a problem. Since I came to the islands, that is. Oh, not when I was a boy in Belgium. I was as good on my feet as anyone in those days, running about the countryside, helping on the farm, driving the cows home at night, skating on the river Dyle. Why, the night before I left home for good I walked fourteen miles to meet my mother at the shrine of Our Lady, to say good-by. Twelve years, I promised her. I didn't keep my promise.

Actually the trouble with my feet started in Puna, my first mission field, on the Big Island, where I'd walk miles over still-warm lava flows, in search of my stray sheep—in those ill-

1

fitting boots. They'd itch and ache and burn—my feet, I mean—and I couldn't get to sleep at night unless I soaked them. After that I had trouble till the day I died.

(Moving to his quarters at the Settlement)

Damien: The day I died—Monday of Holy Week, eighteen eighty-nine. Palm Sunday night, around eleven forty-five, Brother James lights the lantern, wakes up Father Conrardy, the priest who's come to take my place here at the Leper Settlement, and together they go to the church next door. Soon I hear them coming back, Brother James ringing the little altar bell as he walks ahead of Father Conrardy in the dark. Up they come to my room. Brother James holds the napkin under my chin, Father Conrardy says in a sleepy voice, "The body and blood of Christ," and I receive my last communion.

Then Father Conrardy asks if he can have my cassock—threadbare and full of leprosy. What would he do with it? Better I be buried in it.

Next thing I know my roosters are crowing and it's getting light. It's hard to breathe, so Brother James helps me to sit up, and while he's holding me I breathe for the last time. As Brother James bends over to close my eyes, the farewell chant begins outside my door and spreads throughout the Settlement, till every leper knows that Kamiano's spirit has departed.

Brother James brings the basin, washes my body, dresses it in my old cassock, and

(Moving into the neutral area midstage center)

carries it into the church. He puts it in a plain redwood box, and the rest of the day I lie in state. The choir sings my favorite hymns. The lepers file in to say good-bye. This time I have no ointment for their sores, no little jokes to raise their spirits.

By afternoon my sores have crusted over with black scabs. The sickness has consumed me. It has nothing left to feed upon.

Toward evening, Father Conrardy helps Brother James dress me in my vestments. They light the candles and tiptoe out. I am alone. Everything is quiet—except the pounding of the surf and the everlasting whine of Mr. Clifford's barrel organ. That kind man brought it all the way from London, hoping it would amuse us. It has—beyond all expectations. The children wind it up and let it go and are eternally surprised when it makes music of itself. After a while it stops and there is nothing but the surf.

The Requiem Mass next day—with Father Conrardy at the altar—is much the same as those I've celebrated for other lepers, almost three thousand of them. Comforting the mourners, interceding for the dead, the choir pleading: "Eternal rest give unto them, O Lord, and let perpetual light shine upon them. May they rest in peace."

At last eight lepers lift the coffin to their shoulders and Blind Petero's fife and drum corps lead the procession to the cemetery. You know, sorrow at a leper's passing is tempered with gratitude for his release, so Petero's music is anything but sad—actually more like picnic music—as we move to the new grave under the hala tree where I spent my first night at the Settlement.

Young boys from the orphanage stand four deep around the open grave. One suddenly breaks ranks and climbs into the tree. Then the first shovelful of dirt.

For sixteen years I've been sole keeper of this city of the dead. The cemetery, church, and rectory form one enclosure, and it has been my habit to come here after dark to say my beads. Now I have come to rest.

And so I do—for almost half a century. Then, one February day, the black marble stone is rolled away, the ground dug up, the coffin lifted to the surface. A stranger's hands tear away the rotted lid. Lepers I have never known break spontaneously into Hawaiian chants and funeral songs for their dead heroes. And someone cries, "The body is intact, praise God!"

So it is. My hair has grown a little—and my beard. My skin's a deeper bronze, perhaps; the silver rosary is tarnished; the vestments are moldy and the gold embroidery dull. But there are no signs of leprosy. Except for my poor feet, from which a toe or two are missing, the body is intact.

(Coming downstage)

Damien: It had been my wish and my intention to stay here with my lepers. Together we would await the resurrection. Apparently my wish has been forgotten. My body—still in its decaying coffin—is put into a packing case while the priest explains that Father Damien is leaving Kalawao. An airplane waits down at the landing. Why doesn't someone speak up for me? Insist I be allowed to stay?

Fifteen minutes to fly the channel. In my day it took all night, by boat, and whether you were a passenger on deck or a leper in the hold, seasickness was part of it.

The plane puts down in Honolulu; the packing box, draped with the Belgian flag, is transferred to an army caisson. With military escort it moves slowly to its destination: the Fort Street Cathedral.

(Moving upstage to the cathedral area)

Damien: Four days I lie in state—in a koa casket—you know, the kind usually reserved to Hawaiian royalty.

This is my cathedral. The confessionals know my sins, the pews my penances. I was ordained in this cathedral. Here I renewed my vows of poverty, chastity, obedience. Right here, in this sanctuary, I lay under the funeral pall, dying to the world to live in Christ. These hands that have milked cows and curried horses, taken newborn calves, pitched hay, shoveled manure and barnyard waste—these hands were consecrated here. Bishop Maigret took me, a farm boy with only four years religious training—the minimum for priests is ten or more—took me and made a priest of me. "If they won't send me priests," he said, "I'll have to make my own."

When I turned from that altar and saw them at the railing—Hawaiians who only yesterday were worshiping their ancient gods, Kane, Ku, and Lono, when I saw them waiting to receive from me the body and the blood of Christ, my hands trembled, my heart melted like wax, and I knew happiness beyond belief. From that moment I was their servant and their priest.

I attended my first island Mass in this cathedral. We missionaries came straight here from the boat to give thanksgiving for our safe arrival, bedazzled by the sunshine, the flowers, the friendly people chattering in English or Hawaiian, neither of which I then spoke or understood, and a grand cathedral like this where we'd expected none at all.

(Indicating an area just offstage)

Damien: There, in the Bishop's office, I had my first interview with His Excellency. I approached in fear and trembling because of something that had happened at the boat. You see, we've been five months at sea and here we are, starting down the gangplank in Honolulu—six Brothers all in black and ten Sisters all in white. Our feet touch ground. But somehow we can't get our land legs, and the sight of us—sixteen religious staggering like drunken sailors toward our venerable bishop —is too much. I howl with laughter. The boat-day crowds roar back, press up against the ropes, throw flower garlands round my neck. The Bishop, as I come close, is careful not to let his eyes meet mine.

But later, in his office, he laughs. "Nobody threw garlands round my neck when I arrived," he says. "They just deported me. But I came back—aboard a French warship which threatened to shell the city unless freedom of religion were guaranteed and I was allowed to stay. That was thirty years ago. It's still enemy territory, you might say, but that laugh of yours, my boy, helped more than you can realize."

(Back to the neutral area)

Damien: Before the oil of ordination is dry, he ships me off to the Big Island, for a few months in Puna where they hadn't seen a priest in years. Then eight years in Kohala, a parish so large it took two weeks to cover—by canoe, on the back of my poor mule Kapakahi, or on foot. No wonder I started having trouble with my feet.

There were other meetings in the Bishop's office, usually with me begging for money to build chapels and His Excellency grumbling at the cost.

(To the Bishop)

Damien: Yes, Your Excellency, I did send the Mother Superior two hundred pounds of potatoes we have raised. . . . Of course I sent a bill. . . . No, she didn't exactly order them, but everybody needs potatoes and next month when the whalers come the price will double in the market. She got a bargain. . . . For the chapels. . . . Because we need money for a paint bill coming due. . . . Of course chapels don't grow like mushrooms. I've built enough to know. . . . But the chapel's beautiful, Your Excellency. We've made a crucifix six feet high, all decorated with Hawaiian carving. You'll see when you come over for the consecration. . . . Yes, I understand, Your Excellency is busy. . . . Yes, yes, I'm leaving—

(Starts to leave, then turns back)

Damien: You wouldn't be needing any tobacco here at the Mission, would you? Our second crop is coming on. It's beautiful. . . . Yes, yes, I understand. No more shipments of any kind to anybody without a written order. . . . Thank you very much, Your Excellency. Thank you.

(Coming down stage. To the audience)

Damien: I wrote my parents from Kohala:

(Reading from a letter)

Damien: Here I am on an island of volcanoes, one of which, so the Hawaiians believe, is the home of Pele, goddess of eternal fire.

They worship her, and whenever there is an eruption, rush to propitiate her. One man just came by on his way to offer sacrifice, so I seized the opportunity to give him a sermon on the fires of hell. He listened politely, as though he knew more about the fires of hell than I did. There are times when I am tongue-tied before them. I could know all the theology books by heart and still not know what to say. But they like me—call me Kamiano—their way of saying Damien. I keep my body in good shape—and servitude—by spading the vegetables and caring for the lambs, which you will be interested to know, Father, I bought for only two and a half francs apiece. At last I have enough chapels and animals and fields so this year I can spend more time studying and visiting the sick—

(Looking up from the letter)

Damien: I didn't mention the yellow flags. But they were there—on trees and fence posts and even on my chapel door: "All lepers and leper suspects are hereby ordered to report to government health authorities within fourteen days on pain of arrest."

Occasionally I'd see the sheriff's men, with guns and dogs, sniffing about the caves and valleys of my parish. Sometimes I'd hear a distant shot.

One day I came home to find a husband barricaded in my quarters, ready to shoot whoever tried to take his sick wife from him.

One night in the confessional a young boy coughed, hemorrhaged, and covered me with blood.

(Coming even farther downstage)

Damien: Later, in Honolulu, I saw that boy in one of those processions of lepers, down King to Bishop, down Bishop to the waterfront. I saw him torn from his parents' arms and forced into the little boat. I can still hear the father's sobs, see him crouching on the pier, straining for a last glimpse of the little boy he will never see again. I can still hear his mother's farewell chant. All this against an evening sky that seems to mock us with its beauty. What could I do to comfort them but promise that one day I would go to Moloka'i and see their son?

(Returning to the cathedral area)

Damien: There came a time, much later, when I wasn't welcome in this cathedral. After the new Bishop took over. Not only because I had become a leper—that I could understand, but because —Oh, well, never mind. It's over now. Sixty years have passed and here I am—back in my cathedral, and obviously once more in favor. All kinds of dignitaries are filing past the koa casket. A solemn Pontifical Mass is being celebrated, and the Bishop is saying extravagant things about me and reading a message from the Vatican. Now I understand what this is all about: it seems my native country, Belgium, wants me to come home.

(Making the sign of the Cross)

Damien: Go. The Mass is ended.

(Coming downstage right. To the audience)

Damien: The koa casket is carried from the cathedral. The army caisson is loaded and the military procession moves down Bishop Street to King, across King and on down Bishop to the pier where a white ship waits to receive me into her hold. The military band begins its dirge but I—I hear the anguished farewell chant, the cries of lepers as small boats ferry them to a vessel farther out, waiting—as my boat waits—to receive them into her hold, to carry them to Moloka'i.

(Looking out over the audience)

Damien: Moloka'i. Usually it's no trick at all to see her silhouette on the horizon. Today the light's not right. Never mind. In a little while we'll pass quite close enough to see her clearly.

(To the audience)

8

Damien: The first time I saw Moloka'i—the Grey Island as the lepers called it—was from the railing of the ship that brought me to the islands. St. Patrick's Day, 1864, the *R. M. Wood,* five months out of Bremerhaven, entering Hawaiian waters under full sail, sweeps past the other islands till it comes close enough to Moloka'i that I can see a part of it distinctly. A narrow, sour tongue of land sticks out into the sea—the loneliest, most useless piece of land you can imagine. Barren, rock-strewn, wind-whipped—I still find it unbelievable that I could pass so close without some premonition of what it would become: a place of horror, a dumping ground for lepers, the saddest spot on earth.

Of course I had no way of knowing that while we were still two months at sea a doctor in Honolulu had declared: "I take this opportunity to bring before the public a subject of great importance. I mean, of course, the rapid spread of that new disease called by the natives *mai pake.* It is, ladies and gentlemen, true Oriental leprosy, and it will be the duty of the next legislature to take some measures—effective but humane—by which may be accomplished the segregation of all those afflicted."

(Pause)

Damien: From opposite directions, we—leprosy and I—had come to the Sandwich Islands. Contemporaries, you might say, although leprosy was old as time when it arrived and I was barely twenty-four.

(Pause)

Damien: The military dirge comes to an end. A farewell chant starts softly, then fills the air.

Am I remembering? Or hearing it again?

Is it for lepers long ago? Is it for me? But I am out of time— the chants, the boats, the two processions merge, become the same forever. One could not be without the other.

The chant comes to an end. Airplanes cut the sky to ribbons. The koa casket goes aboard. The whistle blows. The white ship, impatient to be off, pulls from her slip and moves out into the channel.

Along the shore, off to the left, half hidden in a grove of palm trees, is the government building that housed the agency entrusted with taking measures—effective but humane—toward segregation of the lepers: The Board of Health.

(Moving downstage left, to the Board of Health area)

Damien: In all good faith they made those yellow flags and nailed them up throughout the kingdom, on trees and posts and sides of buildings—even on the chapel doors of my Kohala Mission.

In all good faith, I'm sure, they bought that sour tongue of land I first saw from the ship. That natural prison, surrounded on three sides by vicious surf and on the fourth by sheer black cliffs that stopped prevailing winds and made them dump their rain; that shut out the sun at noon so the land lay half a day in shadow. ''The place without a sunset,'' the lepers called it.

In all good faith that government body rounded up the lepers —at gunpoint when necessary—and shipped them off with a pair of pants or a cotton dress and a promise of daily rations to supplement what it was hoped the lepers themselves would produce.

In all good faith they called an empty wooden building a hospital and promised to staff it and stock it with supplies.

Effective? Yes. It got the lepers out of circulation so the foreign population could relax.

Humane? No! It was a barbarous method of isolation. That tongue of land became a living graveyard. Can you imagine hundreds—sometimes as many as a thousand—lepers, crowded six, eight, ten, into stinking one-room windowless shacks? Can you imagine a community of the living dead, without a doctor or a nurse? No resident police, no law, no work, no comfort, and no hope. As for the hospital—an empty building where the sickest ones lay on the bare floor in their own filth and waited. But no one came—except the flies by day and the rats by night to feast upon their sores.

Some of the more able-bodies lepers, determined to wrest the last bit of pleasure from their lives gathered in a separate place, dubbed the Village of the Fools, brewed liquor from the roots of plants and spent their days and nights drinking, gambling, whoring, and boasting, *"Aole kanawai ma keia wahi"* —in this place there is no law! And raiding the rest of the Settlement—stealing little girls and boys to use as slaveys or to satisfy their lust.

(Moving downstage center, pointing)

Damien: There—off to the right—that's Moloka'i, its harborless coast, its steep black cliffs that plunge straight down into the sea.

The *second* time I saw Moloka'i was the day before Easter, 1873. A cattle boat en route from Maui to Honolulu, Bishop Maigret and I aboard, stops long enough to land some lepers and fifty head of cattle in its hold. Lepers from the Settlement crowd the landing.

(Moving down the runway, looking upward)

Damien: Look at them! Not one or two or three, but hundreds! In varying stages of corruption, as if the grave has given up its dead. Walking, limping, crawling; they even come in wheelbarrows. Maimed and twisted bodies, sunken faces, missing limbs, maggot-bloated sores. How, dear God, can such things be? I cannot bear to look at them and yet I cannot tear my eyes away as they reach out their rotting arms to welcome new lepers to this place of horror. And they are singing—singing!

Leprosy and I are face to face at last.

(Turning to the neutral area, midstage left)

Damien: The Catholic lepers are gathered round the Bishop, begging him to send a priest—not four on a rotating basis as His Excellency proposes—but one to live among them, to call them by their names, to be a father to them. And he is telling them he cannot ask that sacrifice of anyone. And still they beg.

(To the Bishop)

Damien: They are right, Your Excellency. They must have one priest who belongs to them. To prove to them that God has not forgotten them. I suffer if I go a week without confession. They must go months—years—without confession and the Mass. They must face death without the sacraments. . . . You don't have to ask, Your Excellency. I want to be their priest. I beg to stay.

(To the audience)

Damien: Impetuosity, the Bishop says. Unbalanced generosity. Overreaction to so much brutal suffering. If it had been right, and practical, he'd have sent someone long ago. He would have come himself. Others, before me, have volunteered, but they have been denied. No one, no one, he says, can put aside all human considerations and live—the one clean man—among a thousand lepers.

I don't seem to hear what he is saying. I only see their need and know what I must do.

You see, a man enters the religious life in answer to a "call." Later, if he is lucky, he receives a "call within a call," he finds the niche that he was meant to fill.

This is my niche. This is what I was meant to do. This is why I was born.

So, like the stubborn Fleming that I am, I stick to my guns until His Excellency finally says—God help us both—that if I promise to be prudent I may stay as long as my devotion dictates. That's all I ask—to stay as long as my devotion dictates.

(Calling out to the lepers)

Damien: You have your priest! Do you hear? I am to be your priest. My name is Kamiano. Confessions this afternoon, all night if necessary. And Easter Mass at sunrise!

(To the audience)

Damien: Next morning, while it is still dark, the little church starts filling up with—God forgive me—creatures from a nightmare, limping, shuffling, coughing, spitting, touching with the fingers they have left the rosaries hung round their necks. They keep on coming till the church is filled, up to the railing. They crowd the window sills, the doorways; they fill the church to overflowing, not only with their corrupting bodies, not only with the stench, but with a sadness so unbearable I stand there dumb. The vomit rises in my throat. I choke it back. They kneel and wait, and finally, in a voice I have never heard before, I say the words: *In nomine Patris, et Filii, et Spiritus Sancti.* Amen.

I still remember that first Sunday. I remember going from shack to flimsy shack, visiting people too sick to leave their mats, appalled at so much concentrated misery. I remember wondering how a few leaves from the castor oil plant, tied together with tough grass and anchored to a crumbling stone wall, could provide as much shelter as they did.

I remember someone showing me the shack where Hua, the kahuna, lived. While we were there she came outside and pointed to a formation in the clouds—like a calabash mouth downward—and said it meant the king would die and Emma would be queen and she would let the lepers all go home.

And I remember a young woman in a dirty bathrobe sort of garment telling me she's cold, then opening up her bathrobe to show me she has nothing underneath.

Then there is the man who comes from one of the shacks, carrying a large bundle of dirty rags. He puts the bundle in the wheelbarrow, pushes it to the empty jail house, and shakes it till the dirty rags roll out. I see the bundle move; I hear it groan; I watch it pull itself into the doorway, and lie face down to die.

Later two lepers come, roll the bundle over, tie it to a pole—hands and feet like a luau pig—then take it to the cemetery and bury it in a shallow grave.

And I remember my first night, under the tree there in the cemetery, with rats and scorpions and centipedes to share my vigil, and the sound of wild pigs at that shallow grave, eating their fill.

It was three whole days before I could look at some of the lepers without revulsion. Weeks before I could endure the graveyard smell.

A visiting doctor or agent of the Board of Health would always put a piece of camphor in a handkerchief and tie it round his neck, and every now and then he'd spray himself with camphor liquid. I chose a pipe. And strong black coffee.

The first few weeks I camped outdoors—

(Moving to his quarters)

Damien: Eventually we built my quarters—the more able-bodied lepers and I. Ambrose made that window frame. He'd never touched a tool before. Now they feel the place is theirs somehow. They come here in the evenings, go out there on the lanai with their guitars and sing and play, and in the dark forget that they are lepers.

There was no water at the Settlement. We had to carry it long distances in dirty oil cans and let it stand for days. I couldn't wash my hands or soak my feet without robbing someone of his drinking water. So I roamed the hills for days until I found a place where we could build a reservoir. Some of the lepers helped me lay the pipes and we had running water!

The day my quarters were finished three women, Malia, Philomela, and Elikapeka, said they wanted to keep house for me. Their leper husbands were dead. They themselves were clean. When I hesitated, Philomela laughed. *"Manuahi,* Kamiano. Like you—we work for free."* How could I refuse? I can still hear them laughing at me.

I can hear their scornful laughter, too, when my enemies started peddling scandalous stories about me.

(Crossing over to speak to the Bishop)

Damien: Yes, Your Excellency, I do leave my door open and the light burning all night. . . . Because a priest can do no less. . . . Yes, I leave it open to women as well as men—they get sick and frightened, too. . . . Whoever comes to me comes as Christ, Your Excellency knows that. . . . What do I care what the gossips say? . . . Yes, I rub ointment on their sores with my bare hands. . . . What would Your Excellency have me do? Attend only to the men and boys? Leave the medicine on the gatepost as visiting doctors do? Talk to my lepers through closed windows? Exhort them from the pulpit but never chat with them in private? I'm not an agent of the Board of Health, Your Excellency. I am their priest. Their father in Christ. I'm there to comfort them, to win their hearts and souls. . . .

Yes, I did promise to be prudent, and in my own way I am prudent. Since I am there to comfort Christ in them I am prudent never to let even a shadow of fear or disgust come between us; never to let there be anything but love. . . . Your Excellency, I don't quarrel with other people's ideas of prudence; let no one quarrel with mine. . . .

Yes, I do share my pipe with them. When we're together of an evening, and I light my pipe, and one of them wants a puff or two, can I refuse? Can I, Your Excellency? . . . Yes, I've thought of that. . . . If it is God's will, I am prepared. . . .

By remembering that those worm-infested ulcers are the wounds of Christ—that's how I manage to go on from day to day. . . . If that's the way Your Excellency sees it, then I suppose I am a fool.

(He kneels abruptly to kiss the ring, turns to go, then turns back)

Damien: Yes, Your Excellency?

(Kneeling once more to kiss the ring)

Damien: Thank you, Your Excellency. Thank you very much.

(To the audience)

Damien: His Excellency said he meant I was a fool for Christ.

Intermission

16

ACT TWO

Stage lights come up. Damien is sitting in his rocking chair, smoking, reading a letter. He comes downstage.

(To the audience)

Damien: Ever since Christ touched him and made him clean we've had the leper on our conscience. That's the only explanation for the cries of praise and wonder when word went round the lepers had a priest.

It's easy enough to deal with people when they praise you to your face. I'd just interrupt and tell them something they could do to help. Remind the candy man that leper children still liked candy. Suggest to the baker that a barrel of cookies wouldn't be refused. Tell rich men's wives that leper girls could use scraps of their fine cloth to make dresses for their dollies—that is, if they had the dollies.

I even told the Bishop about Blind Petero and his fife and drum corps; how leprosy could destroy Petero's eyesight but not his love of making music, how we'd made instruments out of scraps of sheet iron so they could play for funerals and weddings, and at the landing when new lepers came. To make sure His Excellency wouldn't forget I made a silly joke about sheet iron music. You should have seen Petero when those instruments arrived. He felt them all over with his hands, held them to his cheek, tears in his poor blind eyes.

Yes, it's easy to handle people when they praise you to your face, but when they put things about you in the paper—

(To the Bishop)

17

Damien: This is absurd, Your Excellency. Ridiculous! The Hero of Moloka'i! A Priest's Renunciation! And this from the prime minister!

(Reading)

Damien: "I've had my dreams of service to mankind, but none sublime as Father Damien's renunciation. Without for one moment subscribing to his religion, I can say this: He is a martyr. A true Christian martyr."

(To the Bishop)

Don't they understand? I'm only doing my priestly duty as I see it. Can't Your Excellency do something to stop this silly chatter? . . . I want privacy. I want to live quietly with my lepers, doing whatever I can to prove to them that God has not forgotten them. . . . Your Excellency, leprosy I can face—it corrupts only the body, but praise like this breeds pride and pride corrupts the soul. . . . I know, I know—all praise belongs to God, but what if I forget? What if I let such stuff corrupt my soul? . . .

Is it a matter of obedience, Your Excellency? . . . Then you must pray for me. Constantly. And ask others to do the same—for I am very much afraid.

(To the audience)

Damien: His Excellency said the Church Council had discussed the—the uproar, and could find no *human* explanation for it. Could it be the hand of God? Could it be the leper's time had come and I was to bring the leper's cause before the world? Whatever it was, he said, I must give up my wish for privacy. I must suffer this stuff gladly. The more reporters wrote about the lepers the better.

Oh, I had my detractors, too. They said I was a leper when I went to Kalawao but concealed my condition to make myself a hero. They said I collected money for the lepers and poured it into the coffers of the church.

They say I am a coarse and dirty man, and—among other things in which I dare say there is a grain of truth—that I am awkward, undisciplined, long-winded, hot-tempered—

Hot-tempered! The Board of Health would certainly say aye to that.

You see, the day after that first big blow on Moloka'i, when half our flimsy shacks were literally carried out to sea, I took the boat to Honolulu. At the Chancery they told me His Excellency was calling on the president of the Board of Health. So I went over there—

(Crossing to stage left. To the Bishop and the president of the Board of Health)

Damien: Your Excellency, they said I'd find you here. Mr. President . . . I did knock and no one answered. . . . I heard voices so I came in. . . . Yes, I realize I am intruding, but it's most important. . . . Even if I am unwelcome I must report. The night before last . . . the night before last . . . Your Excellency, ask him to let me speak. . . . The night before last a hurricane and waterspout demolished half our shacks and we need help at once. Lepers too sick to move are lying on the ground, completely at the mercy of the elements. We need food and clothing, medicine, everything. Eventually we will need materials to replace the shacks, but for the moment. . . . No, the Captain can't give you a report. He didn't even come ashore. He thought it best for me to come. . . . No, Mr. President, no! I am not here in the capacity of a Catholic missionary priest. I am here as the self-appointed representative of every leper in that—that charnelhouse you call the Settlement. . . . It is a charnelhouse, Your Excellency. With patients dying every day—not from leprosy but from neglect. Anemia from lack of proper nourishment, dysentery from contaminated food and water, bronchial pneumonia from lack of proper clothing. Do you know, Mr. President, how long it is since most of them have tasted milk? I protest such gross neglect. . . . No, Your Excellency. . . . No, Mr. President. Not until I'm through. The shacks will have to be replaced with wooden cottages—on trestles—proof against the kind of storm

19

that strikes the Settlement. . . . I can give you an esti-
mate. . . . Well, if the Board can't help us, we can ask elsewhere. . . . My haphazard begging makes you *look* niggardly?
Is six dollars per leper per year enough to provide clothing,
even for a person in perfect health? Could you exist on sour
poi and scraps of putrid meat for weeks on end? Sometimes
not even that, when stores are dumped overboard because of
heavy seas, and starving lepers must stand on the shore and
watch the sea devour them. As for that shack you call a
hospital—

He's gone, Your Excellency. I know. . . . I know. I'm sorry. I
swore when I came through that door I wouldn't lose my temper, but when he stood there, well-fed, pink-cheeked, sancti-
monious, and told me I wasn't welcome—I'm sorry, Your Excellency. Very sorry. I don't know what to say. . . . You think
I said it rather well? . . . You're not angry with me? . . . I
know my temper is a serious flaw—

(To the audience)

Damien: His Excellency said something which was to comfort me the
rest of my life, though I try never to use it as an excuse. He said
that God seemed to put such flaws in his most zealous priests
—to keep them humble.

Oh, the gossips had their day, too. They said I slept with
women. It wasn't true. I kept my vow of chastity. Not that I
was never tempted—

(Remembering)

Damien: The night of Sammy's wedding. Sammy was the son of a
nonleper family living outside the Settlement. It was an evening wedding—flowers, music, full moon, a luau afterward. I
didn't have a horse at that time; it was too far to walk back to
the Settlement, so I planned to stay all night with Sammy's
parents.

We all slept on the floor in one big room. After the father had
blown out the candle and everything was still, someone un-

rolled a sleeping mat alongside mine and reached out a hand to touch me. It was the young daughter of the family.

I got up and went outside. The moon was full. It was cool and fragrant—and every instinct in me was alive. I got to the stone wall, then turned around. She was standing in the doorway, in the moonlight, naked.

I walked all night and reached the Settlement by morning. I could still see her standing in the doorway. After that, she'd come between me and the pages of my breviary. Sometimes I'd see her—her body on the Cross.

I had no one to talk to—no other priest. When I did get to Honolulu to confess, the Bishop told me that strong men turn temptation to their profit. After that, whenever she appeared to me I'd say out loud, "God alone is worthy of my love. He is my troth forever." That's how I kept my vow of chastity.

(To the audience)

Damien: You see, when a priest works alone, with no companion priest, he frequently must go weeks or months without confession. This was a great hardship for me, and when I went to Moloka'i it was understood that—so long as I remained in health—I would go to Honolulu once a month to stay over night at the Mission.

Abruptly, without warning, the Board of Health informed me I was never again to leave the Settlement for any purpose whatsoever. I could, if I wished, declare myself a leper and remain confined as other lepers, or I could leave the Settlement for good.

(To the Bishop)

Damien: Doctors and clergy aren't subject to such restrictions. This is a trap, Your Excellency. They want to get rid of me. They know I can't live without the sacraments. They want me to leave the Settlement of my own accord; to make a laughingstock of myself, my Order, and my Church. Then, without the leper

21

priest to write about, reporters will stop airing the awful truths about the Settlement. . . . Yes, Your Excellency, my devotion still dictates that I stay . . . but there are laws of man and laws of God, and whenever the two conflict I follow the laws of God. I am entitled to the sacraments. I will continue to come and go and ask no odds of any man. . . . Let them arrest me. Let them throw me into jail.

(To the audience)

Damien: They do arrest Father Aubert. You see, he knows what the sacraments mean to me, so he disguises himself as a ruffian, comes from Maui—not directly to the Settlement but to the town up there—and in the dead of night slides down that cliff where even in broad daylight men and animals have fallen to their death—just so I can make confession. He climbs back up the cliff by morning, but the sheriff's men are waiting for him at the top.

A few weeks later a leper boat arrives from Maui. I learn from the new lepers that my Provincial is aboard. When he doesn't come ashore while they're unloading, as he usually does, I grab a landing craft and paddle out.

(Coming down the runway)

Damien: There he is at the railing. He tells me he's forbidden to come ashore so I start up the accommodation ladder. The Captain shouts, "Stand back. By order of the Board of Health!" I beg five minutes with my Provincial. The Captain shakes his head, so Father Modeste leans over the railing, makes the sign of the Cross, and I—kneeling in the little boat, with captain, crew, and passengers looking on—make my confession:

(Kneeling and making the sign of the Cross)

Damien: Bless me, Father, for I have sinned. Since my last confession I have completely lost my temper seven times and spoken rudely and with anger to men from the Board of Health. I have accused them of—murdering my lepers by deliberate and intentional neglect. And I have not apologized because I believe

22

it to be true. At such times I am so consumed with anger I am unfit to stand before the altar.

Three days ago, at the Village of the Fools, I raised my stick against a man. I caught him using Little Boy Kimi—using him —using him to satisfy his lust. The man defied me, rushed me, rubbed his leprous stump across my face, and I forgot myself and beat him with my stick until the blood came. I told him if he ever touched a child that way again I myself would tie the millstone round his neck and throw him into the sea. What else can I do to protect the children?

(Sound of a ship's whistle. To the audience)

Damien: The ship's whistle drowns out my words, but my Provincial motions to me and I go on and on until my heart is empty. As the ship begins to move away I see him raise his hand and I feel the peace of absolution.

(Coming down the runway, to downstage center. To the audience)

Damien: Eventually, at the suggestion of the French consul, the order is modified and, as long as I remain in health, I am free to come and go at will.

(Pause)

Damien: The years go by—five, ten, eleven, twelve, and my relations with the Board of Health go up and down. Sometimes they criticize my work; sometimes they praise it; sometimes they even flatter me, saying I am the strongest moral influence at the Settlement.

When the resident superintendent dies they offer me his job. Ten thousand dollars a year! At the time I take their offer at face value.

(Sitting on the small box stage center. To members of the Board of Health)

Damien: Thank you, gentlemen, but I must decline. Some priests, as you know, take a vow of poverty. . . . But, gentlemen, I don't want to get around it. . . . But I don't want less personal contact with the lepers. My work *is* personal contact. . . . More money? Gentlemen, if it were money keeping me here I wouldn't stay five minutes. It's service to the lepers keeps me here. . . . Yes, I'd still be serving them, but for a salary, don't you see? I'd be a hireling and everything I've tried to do up to this moment would be wasted. My own mother wouldn't acknowledge me her son if I took money for this work. . . . But Christ told his disciples to go forth without gold or purse, to heal the sick and cleanse the leper and He would provide. He has provided. I am penniless, yet I have a warehouse full of gifts from strangers for my lepers. Do you think I could betray that mystery? . . . I'm sorry, gentlemen, that you don't understand.

(To the audience)

Damien: As I said, at the time I took their offer at face value. As things turned out, I'm more inclined to think—well, let's put it this way: It wasn't my meager talents as administrator they wanted. It was another try to make me an employee of the Board of Health.

Life at the Settlement was not all misery. A leper takes a long time dying and there is some happiness along the way. Can you imagine how Malia feels when I fix her up with sticks for these two missing fingers and she finds she can still play the church organ? She touches the keys, the music comes, and the choir sings out with joy enough to break your heart: "Holy God, we praise thy name. Lord of All, we bow before thee—"

I liked the mornings best, when the young ones went racing up and down the one main street, laughing, shouting, urging their horses on. One day I'm carrying the body of a woman to her coffin in the church and it's half an hour we wait there in the sun until it's safe to cross.

Even a funeral is a kind of celebration. The procession to the cemetery, Blind Petero's fife and drum corps, the choirs singing, the rival burial societies with their different-colored sashes and banners—well, it isn't dreary, I can vouch for that.

(Going to his quarters)

Damien: There is an endless stream of letters filled with kindness—and all those gifts I mentioned. Some distinguished visitors find their way to Moloka'i: Princess Lili'uokalani, in great distress, promises to do whatever she can for her stricken people. Charles Warren Stoddard comes from California, and Edward Clifford from London, and both write books about the Settlement. Stoddard calls his *The Lepers of Molokai,* and I read favorite passages to the children. They recognize themselves and laugh with joy.

(Reading to the children)

Damien: "The first glimpse of the Settlement might lead a stranger to pronounce it the prettiest village in all the islands. Its single street is bordered by neat whitewashed cottages—"

(To the audience)

Damien: I forgot to tell you—after that big blow we did build those cottages. Three hundred of them, whitewashed inside and out, with windows in them. We planted sweet potatoes in the back, against the time when there was no poi, and flowers in the front, and, when the first red ginger bloomed like blood against the whitewashed wall, the whole Settlement turned out to see.

(Back to the children)

Damien: Didn't they? Which one? . . . the part about the chickens? Here it is: "Father Damien brought a handful of corn and scattering a little on the ground gave a peculiar cry. In a moment, the chickens flocked from all quarters; they lit upon his arms, fed from his hands, they fought for footing upon his shoulders, even his head—covering him with feathers and caresses. He stood knee-deep in them." . . . More? The part about the Mass? I'm not going to read all that!

(Reading)

Damien: "After the Mass a brief instruction period, then the priest says pau . . . and everybody leaves. One little boy forgot his cap and I ran after him—"

That was you, wasn't it Keola? That's why you wanted me to read that part.

(To the audience)

Damien: Stoddard goes on to say, "I find it strange their hearts are still comparatively gay." Stoddard is right. Our hearts *are* comparatively gay because deep down inside we've come to know our lives have meaning. We are a concentrated cry for help. Our voices are being heard. We are a symbol to all lepers. We have escaped from our degrading exile. No Board of Health can ever again confine us to this sour tongue of land.

(A ship's whistle is heard in the distance)

Damien: Hear that? Ships from around the world salute us as they pass —even in the dead of night.

(Pause)

Damien: But there was always the question in people's minds: Is Damien himself immune to leprosy?

The answer comes one evening in December 1884, after twelve years at the Settlement. There have been warnings: spots here on my arm, but a little corrosive sublimate clears them up. Severe pain in my left leg, but Dr. Trousseau says it's sciatica, and eventually it goes away. My face has turned a deeper bronze, but then I run around bareheaded all the time. I go up there in the sun and wind to patch the church roof.

This particular evening I am writing to my mother on her eighty-third birthday. I recall my promise to come home in twelve years. Suddenly a terrible homesickness comes over me. I want so much to hear my mother's voice, to breathe some good clean Flemish air, to walk in snow, and hear the sleigh bells. I put the letter aside, get up, find my breviary, pour the boiling water into the basin, and sit down to soak my feet, my left one first. I find my place, begin to read, then start to put my right foot in. But I've forgotten to pour in the cold. I jerk my right foot out, then look down at my left. The skin is hanging from the flesh, the blisters are already forming. But there is no pain—

(Crossing to the cathedral area, he rings the church bell. Speaking to his lepers)

Damien: My dear children, I have called you here to tell you something that concerns us all. From the day I came to live among you I have always said "we lepers" because I wanted to be one of you. God has seen fit to grant my wish. Now I can never leave you—for I am in truth a leper. Receive me. Rejoice with me and remember always: whatever happens, God knows best. If it is any comfort to you, I'm not taken by surprise. I think I've always known—from that first night under the hala tree. Yes, I think I knew it then.

Now, we lepers will celebrate the Mass together. Pray that we go on, that we will have time to finish what we have started, particularly the dormatories for the orphans.

(To the audience)

Damien: My leprosy is speedily confirmed—not only by the doctors in Honolulu, but by the look in people's eyes, the camphor in the handkerchief, hands clasped carefully behind the back. I am no longer Father Damien—I am a contaminated animal, a leper.

My Provincial writes to me like this:

(Reading from a letter)

Damien: "If you insist on coming to Honolulu to try the new cure, you must go to the Receiving Station, where you will go to the lepers' chapel but not say Mass, for neither Father Clement

27

nor I will consent to celebrate Mass with the same vestments you have used, and the Sisters will refuse Holy Communion from your hands.''

(To the audience)

Damien: He's right, of course, but did he have to spell it out for me?

(Back to the letter)

Damien: "Your attitude indicates that you possess neither delicacy of feeling nor charity toward your neighbor—that you think only of yourself. Your very words reveal your egoism. . . .''

(Crumples the letter and throws it away. To the audience)

Damien: Doesn't he understand? I am thinking of my lepers. If the cure helps me, then I can bring it back to them.

There are others who are kinder. The Captain of the boat, for instance, the one who wouldn't give me five minutes alone with my Provincial—he invites me to his cabin for a glass of wine.

There are things worse to bear than leprosy. When a man gives his whole life to one preoccupation, then toward the end doubts arise. Doubts—like maggots in a leper's sore.

You see, when it becomes known I am a leper, reporters have a field day. Banner headlines: Soldier of Christ Struck Down! Damien Hangs on the Leper's Cross! And column after column about the Settlement, the lepers, and myself. Letters of love and sympathy pour in—and gifts of money, thirty thousand gold francs in all.

But the King, the government, the Board of Health, the Mission are all offended. The articles don't mention them. When I try to explain I'm not responsible for the articles, they tell me I am drunk with pride, so drunk I'm dangerous, unfit to handle all that money. In future the Board of Health will receive all financial gifts—even those addressed personally to me.

What does a government clerk know about a leper's needs?

When I protest the new bishop advises an examination of conscience.

Have I really sought to do God's will, or were my ceaseless activities, my unbalanced generosity, my caprices of self-will, my stubborn lack of prudence merely following the bent of my own temperament?

Have I deceived myself?

Have I a secret vanity that feeds on notoriety?

Have I let this prominence and praise corrupt me?

Even this I understand, but when the new bishop chides me for showing no distinction between Catholic and non-Catholic lepers—

(To the Bishop)

Damien: You don't ask a leper if he's a Catholic, Your Excellency. If a dying woman tells you she can't bear the thought of being devoured by pigs when she is dead, you don't ask if she's a Catholic. You make a coffin for her and when she dies you bury her and commend her soul to God, quite sure that He won't ask her either.

When a leper, on his deathbed, cries out for absolution, you go to him and all distinctions vanish as you inhale his fetid breath and hear his dying words, and in the name of Christ forgive him, regardless. . . . Oh, no, Your Excellency. . . . No!

(To the audience)

Damien: I was—His Excellency said—a defective priest. There are worse things than leprosy.

          (Pause)

Damien: Well, I've talked so much we're well past Moloka'i. She's back there in the mist. We're in deep water now. The sea is calm; the ship is steady. But not for long; a violent storm churns up the waves, tossing our vessel like a toy ship from crest to crest.

          One day we stop while the koa casket is put aboard another ship. The voices of the sailors are familiar. No, not the voices —the language. It is a Belgian ship—the crew are speaking my mother tongue.

          At last one morning we drop anchor. The koa casket goes ashore. Trumpets blare, cannon boom, all of Antwerp's bells ring out, and King Leopold himself steps forward to salute.

          I am on Belgian soil once more.

          All kinds of ceremonies, including a solemn Pontifical Mass.

          Then at last, toward evening, the traditional hearse receives the coffin, and drawn by six white horses, moves slowly south- ward in the direction of Louvain.

          Somewhere around midnight we pass my father's farm, in the moonlight looking much as I remember it—except for a few more outbuildings perhaps, a few more noisy dogs, and the house itself looks awkward somehow. Then I remember: when father died Leonce moved his family in with mother and built an upstairs room for me if I came home.

          Look—there's a light on in the parlor—where we used to gather after supper, my father to enter figures in a thin black ledger and my mother to read aloud from a fat black book— *Holy Saints and Martyrs*.

          The thin black ledger and the fat black book—I see it now, the battle they were waging. As soon as mother finished reading about the saints and martyrs in her black book my father would call me over and show me the figures in his black book and tell me how, when I grew up, I'd go into the business and be a grain merchant like himself. That's why he sent me off to school to learn French and mathematics and other things grain merchants need to know.

My mother had a lot of stories about me as a child—the things I did—you know how mothers are. The year the barn was painted, did I daub my hands and feet with red and say I was St. Francis receiving the stigmata? I don't remember.

I do recall the day my older brother Auguste became a priest. Everyone agrees, Auguste was born to be a priest. He's naturally restrained and gentle, but I—well, Auguste was everything I wasn't but longed to be. When I saw him kneel and place his slender hands between the Bishop's, when I heard him take his vows of poverty, chastity, and obedience, in my young and secret heart I took them, too. Before I'd earned a cent I took the vow of poverty. Before I knew what passion was I took the vow of chastity. Before I knew the strength of my own will I'd promised to obey.

The Christmas I was twenty I told my father:

(To his father)

Damien: I don't want to be a grain merchant, Father. . . . I want to be a priest. . . . I know you've counted on me. . . . I know you need me in the business. . . . I know eventually it would be mine—but I don't want it, Father. . . . I know you've already given three children to the church. . . . I have thought it over. . . . I am sure, Father. . . . No! You can't forbid me. It's my vocation. It's God—not you—will tell me what to do.

(To the audience)

Damien: I've spoiled the holidays. Christmas and New Year's come and go and not a word between my father and me. Even on my birthday there's no breakfast-table gift. But he does speak to me. He says he's going into Louvain on business. Would I like

31

to ride in with him? I can visit at the Sacred Hearts House with Auguste until it's time to drive back home.

Auguste seems to be expecting me. He introduces me to Father Wencelas, who also seems to be expecting me. We talk a little, then Father Wencelas nods and says yes, he'll take me as a novice. At dusk my father comes back to shake my hand and then ride home alone.

It's getting light. In a little while we'll reach Louvain and the journey will be over. Off to the left is the shrine. Our Lady of Montagu. That's where we said good-bye—my mother and I— three quarters of a century ago.

(Remembering)

Damien: The candles cast their flickering shadows as my mother's wrinkled fingers slip silently along her beads. She prays for my return. Your prayers are answered, Mother. I have come home.

(To the audience)

Damien: That was the American college of Louvain that we just passed. I was refused admission there because—these are their words on record: Because of rudeness of manner and appearance and gross ignorance of any language save his own—and a little French which he subjects to the most exquisite tortures.

They were right about the language. As for the rudeness of manner and appearance, I told them then, I tell them now: I come of peasant stock. We peasants aren't given to delicate language and fancy manners. We distrust formality. We say what we have to say, do what we have to do. We are what we are. It is our nature and we will face death rather than go against it, because we believe our nature comes from God.

The hearse is slowing to a stop in front of the Sacred Hearts House where my father left me on my twentieth birthday. Priests line the sidewalks—and young boys, too. My heart goes out to them. My novice days were painful. I'd come late to the religious life, with much of the world still clinging to me. I needed something to remind me, so I took my penknife and carved three words—right here—in my new wooden desk—words the hermits in the black book used: silence, recollection, prayer. Father Wencelas, when he discovers it, is appalled. Such "wanton destruction of church property calls for public reprimand." It wasn't my only public reprimand.

Would I have survived without Auguste? Without his gentle but relentless criticism?

(To Auguste)

Damien: I know, Auguste. You've told me that before. . . . I do try. . . . I know I'm clumsy. I know I'm much too sociable for a religious. . . . I talk too much, laugh too loud. Yes, I know I'm much too eager, too hearty, too explosive. There's just too much of me. . . . But I can't be like you, Auguste. . . . I can't be subtle. I have to say what I think. The words come out in spite of me. . . . That's not true—I do try to control my temper. I do pray for a docile heart. . . . I will try to be more restrained . . . but there's one thing I don't understand. You say I must learn to do everything—even good—in moderation. But Christ said we must give *all* for him.

(To the audience)

Damien: One day Father Wencelas tells me—very kindly—that I must not aspire to the priesthood. The most I can expect, he says, is to become a choir or missionary brother. My heart rebels and I give him perfect proof that he is right: I fly into a rage.

Then, a few days later Auguste falls sick and can't go to the Sandwich Islands, so I by-pass Father Wencelas, write to the Father General in Paris begging him to let me take my brother's place. When the Father General writes back and says to let me go, Father Wencelas throws the letter on my desk and shouts, "You're not ready yet. You'll get out there and do more harm than good."

We're in St. Joseph's chapel now. Here I will await the resurrection. It's quiet and peaceful, but I am lonesome for my lepers. With half a world between us, my old doubts return.

(Turning to the cathedral area. Alone with his Lord)

Damien: Did I do more harm than good?

Did I betray you, Lord?

Was I a defective priest?

Was I stubbornly following the bent of my own temperament?

But it was my temperament to seek you with a passion that consumed me. Once I had felt the wound of love there was no other way. You were with me in the lepers' shacks. You let me hear a festering mass of flesh still praise your name. The agonies I consoled, the wounds I nursed were yours . . . the agony and the wounds of Christ. Tell me this is true, Lord. Tell me this is true. One word and all these doubts will vanish like smoke before the wind.

(Pause)

Damien: If it is these doubts that come between us, Lord, then I will cast them out. In your name, Lord, I cast them out. Whatever I have done for good or ill, I am your priest. You are my God. I trust in your prodigious love.

(As the stage lights dim on Damien at the foot of the Cross, the salute of a passing ship is heard in the distance)

END

SOURCES

"Song of the Chanter Ka-'ehu" is reprinted from *The Echo of Our Song: Chants & Poems of the Hawaiians,* translated and edited by Mary K. Pukui and Alfons L. Korn. Copyright © 1973 by The University Press of Hawaii.

FACTS OF FATHER DAMIEN'S LIFE

Newspapers and periodicals of the period.

Vital Jourdain, SS.CC. *The Heart of Father Damien.* Translated by Francis Larkin SS.CC. and Charles Davenport. Milwaukee, Wisconsin: The Bruce Publishing Company, 1955.

Charles Warren Stoddard. *The Lepers of Molokai.* Notre Dame, Indiana: Ave Maria Press, n.d.

DESCRIPTION OF THE LEPER SETTLEMENT

Alfons L. Korn, ed. *News from Molokai: Letters between Peter Kaeo and Queen Emma, 1873-1876.* Honolulu: The University Press of Hawaii, 1976.

PHOTO CREDITS

Frontispiece: Father Damien. Courtesy of the Damien Museum, Honolulu.

Terence Knapp as Damien: Courtesy of Hawaii Public Television, Joe Konno, photographer.

Set: Courtesy of Richard C. Mason.